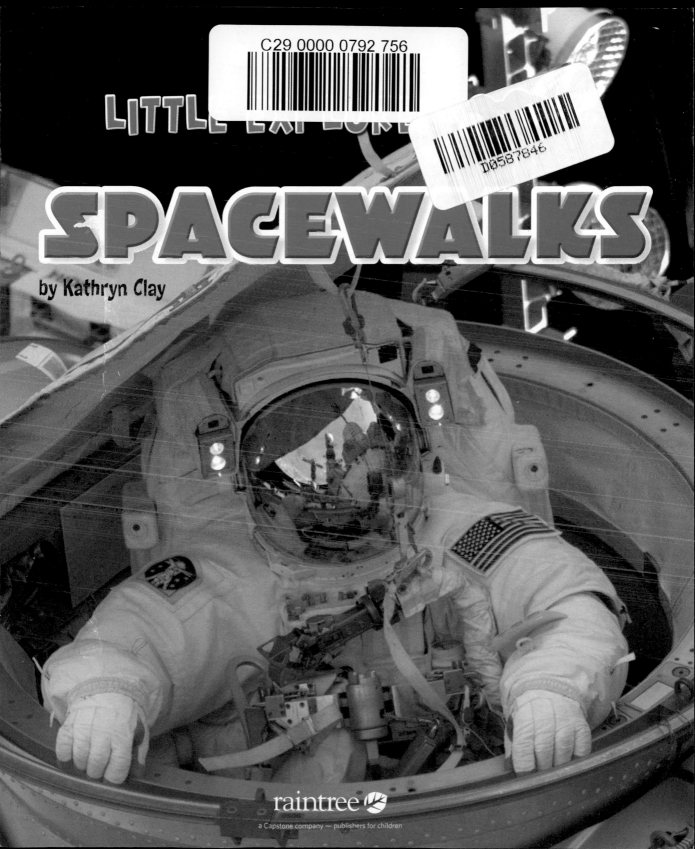

LITTLE EXPLORE

SPACEWALKS

by Kathryn Clay

raintree

a Capstone company — publishers for children

Raintree is an imprint of Capstone Global Library Limited, a company incorporated in England and Wales having its registered office at 264 Banbury Road, Oxford, OX2 7DY – Registered company number: 6695582

www.raintree.co.uk
myorders@raintree.co.uk

ISBN 978 1 4747 3301 4 (hardback)
21 20 19 18 17
10 9 8 7 6 5 4 3 2 1

ISBN 978 1 4747 3305 2 (paperback)
22 21 20 19 18
10 9 8 7 6 5 4 3 2 1

British Library Cataloguing in Publication Data
A full catalogue record for this book is available from the British Library.

Editorial Credits
Arnold Ringstad, editor; Jake Nordby, designer and production specialist

Our very special thanks to Dr. Valerie Neal, Curator and Chair of the Space History Department at the Smithsonian National Air and Space Museum for her curatorial review. Capstone would also like to thank Kealy Gordon, Smithsonian Institution Product Development Manager, and the following at Smithsonian Enterprises: Christopher A. Liedel, President; Carol LeBlanc, Senior Vice President; Brigid Ferraro, Vice President; Ellen Nanney, Licensing Manager.

Acknowledgements
ESA/NASA, 27; NASA: cover, 1, 3, 4–5, 8, 9, 11 (top), 12, 13, 14, 15 (left), 15 (right), 16 (top), 16 (bottom), 17, 18, 19 (left), 19 (middle), 19 (right), 20, 21, 22, 23, 24, 25, 28–29, 30–31, Neil A. Armstrong, 10–11; Science Source: David Ducros, 26, David Hardy, 29, Detlev van Ravenswaay, 7, RIA Novosti, 6; Shutterstock: gn8, 11 (bottom)

Design Elements: Shutterstock Images: MarcelClemens, Ovchinnkov Vladimir, Shay Yacobinski, Tashal, Teneresa

Printed in the United States of America in North Mankato, Minnesota

Printed and bound in India.

CONTENTS

WHAT IS A SPACEWALK?

Exiting a spacecraft in space is called a spacewalk. More than 200 astronauts have gone on spacewalks.

TOP SPACEWALKERS BY 2016

astronaut	country	number of spacewalks	total time
1. Anatoly Solovyev	Russia	16	82 hours 22 minutes
2. Michael Lopez-Alegria	USA	10	67 hours 40 minutes
3. Jerry L. Ross	USA	9	58 hours 32 minutes
4. John M. Grunsfeld	USA	8	58 hours 30 minutes
5. Richard Mastracchio	USA	9	53 hours 4 minutes

Astronauts perform spacewalks for many reasons. They may test equipment or set up experiments. Sometimes they build space stations. At other times they make repairs.

THE FIRST SPACEWALK

On 18 March 1965, Cosmonaut Alexei Leonov made history. He was the first person to go outside a spacecraft. He stayed connected to it by a tether. For 10 minutes he floated in space.

"It was so quiet I could even hear my heart beat. I was surrounded by stars and was floating without much control. I will never forget the moment."
—Alexei Leonov

There was a problem when Leonov tried to come back inside the spacecraft. The air pressure in Leonov's suit blew it up like a balloon. It was too big to fit through the hatch! He allowed some of the air to leak out. Then he squeezed himself safely inside.

an artist's image of Leonov on his historic spacewalk

THE FIRST U.S. SPACEWALK

The first NASA spacewalk happened three months later. On 3 June 1965, the two astronauts of the Gemini 4 mission circled Earth in their spacecraft. Astronaut Ed White opened the hatch and floated into space. He was attached to the spacecraft by a tether.

NASA stands for National Aeronautics and Space Administration. It is the United States' space agency.

tether

White drifted near the spacecraft for 23 minutes. His suit expanded like Leonov's had. White had trouble moving his arms and legs. But the hatch was easier to enter than the one on Leonov's spacecraft. White reentered without problems.

The spacecraft used for the Gemini missions held two astronauts.

WALKING ON THE MOON: THE FIRST LANDING

Millions of people stared at their TVs on 20 July 1969. Audiences held their breath as the spacecraft *Eagle* landed on the moon. A few hours later, Astronauts Neil Armstrong and Buzz Aldrin left *Eagle* and became the first people to walk on the moon. They did not need tethers. They could walk back to their lander.

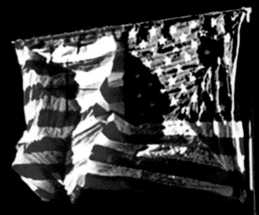

Armstrong and Aldrin planted an American flag on the moon.

The moon has lower gravity than Earth. A lower gravity means people weigh less. Armstrong and Aldrin bounced around on the surface.

Aldrin climbs out of *Eagle*.

"That's one small step for a man, one giant leap for mankind."—Neil Armstrong

WALKING ON THE MOON: MORE EXPLORATIONS

Five more crews landed on the moon in the next three years. Walking was difficult in the space suit. The astronauts found other ways to move around in low gravity. The best was a slow hop from one foot to the other.

PEOPLE WHO HAVE WALKED ON THE MOON	
mission	astronauts
Apollo 11	Neil Armstrong and Buzz Aldrin
Apollo 12	Pete Conrad and Alan Bean
Apollo 14	Alan Shepard and Edgar Mitchell
Apollo 15	David Scott and James Irwin
Apollo 16	John Young and Charles Duke
Apollo 17	Eugene Cernan and Harrison Schmitt

Astronaut John Young leaps in the low gravity of the moon.

Astronauts used a small car called a rover on three of their missions to the moon. The suited astronauts could drive it far from their lander. It let them explore more of the moon.

Astronaut Eugene Cernan drives the rover.

FIXING THE HUBBLE SPACE TELESCOPE

The Hubble Space Telescope was launched into space in 1990. Scientists hoped it would send back very clear pictures. But all the images appeared blurry. Something was not right. In 1993 astronauts were sent to fix it. They flew on the space shuttle *Endeavour*. The astronauts went on five spacewalks. Each one lasted more than six hours. They successfully fixed the telescope.

Spacewalking astronauts work on the Hubble Space Telescope.

HUBBLE SERVICING MISSIONS (SM)

- SM 1 (5 spacewalks): December 1993

- SM 2 (5 spacewalks): February 1997

- SM 3A (3 spacewalks): December 1999

- SM 3B (5 spacewalks): March 2002

- SM 4 (5 spacewalks): May 2009

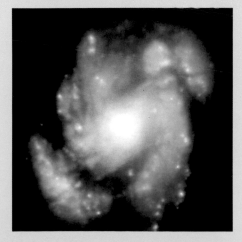

The Hubble spacewalks helped the telescope's images go from blurry (left) to clear (right).

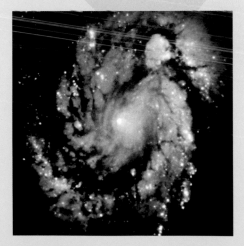

SPACE STATION SPACEWALKS

Astronauts and cosmonauts began building the International Space Station (ISS) in 1998. They connected the first two modules, Zarya and Unity, in December of that year. Astronauts Jerry Ross and James Newman went on three spacewalks to install cables and antennas.

Unity

Zarya

In 2001 Astronaut Chris Hadfield became the first Canadian spacewalker. He spent nearly eight hours connecting power to a robotic arm on the station.

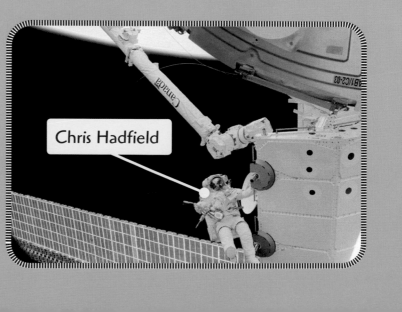

Chris Hadfield

Astronaut Jerry Ross works on connecting the first parts of the ISS.

By 2016 nearly 200 spacewalks had happened at the ISS.

SUITING UP

Astronauts need special suits for spacewalking. The suits keep them safe in space. A suit is basically a one-person spacecraft.

Astronaut Sunita Williams puts on her space suit as she prepares for a spacewalk in 2012.

Gemini programme space suit (1966)

Apollo programme space suit (1972)

Space shuttle/ISS space suit (2003)

There is no air in space. A suit gives an astronaut oxygen to breathe. It protects the astronaut from extreme temperatures, too. The outside of the suit gets hot in sunlight and cold in shadows. Inside, the astronaut stays comfortable.

SPACE SUIT PARTS

Space suits have many parts to keep astronauts safe. Each suit has 14 layers. Some layers keep the astronaut at a comfortable temperature. Others hold in the astronaut's air or protect the suit from damage.

Inside a space suit, astronauts are safe from the dangers of space.

The helmet has a thin layer of gold on the outside. It reflects dangerous rays from the sun. A headset and microphone are inside the helmet. They let astronauts talk to each other. An astronaut also wears a backpack. It holds a battery and tanks of air and water. Switches on the chest let the astronaut control these systems.

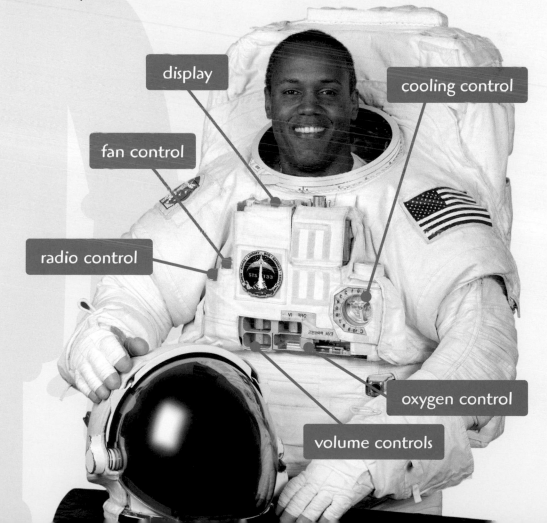

display

cooling control

fan control

radio control

oxygen control

volume controls

SPACEWALK TRAINING

Astronauts spend months training for spacewalks. In space they are weightless. In some ways this feels like being underwater. Spacewalk training is done underwater in a large pool. The pool is in Houston, Texas, U.S.A.

An astronaut is lowered into the training pool.

Divers help astronauts train
underwater for spacewalks.

The pool contains a full-size
model of the ISS. Astronauts
practise the work they will do
on their spacewalks.

The training pool
holds 23 million litres
(6.2 million gallons) of
water. It is the biggest
indoor pool on Earth.

SPACEWALK SAFETY: FLOATING AWAY

Tethers are attached to the space suits. These cords connect to the spacecraft or space station. They keep astronauts from floating away. Astronauts may also be attached to robotic arms.

Tethers are not the only way astronauts stay safe. Their backpacks have thrusters. Astronauts could use them to return to the spacecraft in emergencies.

robotic arm

tether

backpack with thrusters

SPACEWALK SAFETY: SUIT DAMAGE

Floating away is not the only danger during spacewalks. Another concern is flying debris. Tiny pieces of metal or chips of paint move very fast in space. They could damage a suit. Astronauts regularly check for small rips and tears.

Tiny bits of debris can cause lots of damage to spacecraft or space suits.

The suits hold cool water to keep astronauts from overheating. Sometimes this water can leak. In 2013 a leak sprung in Luca Parmitano's suit during a spacewalk. His helmet began to fill with water. Luckily he was able to return to the ship safely and remove his helmet.

Parmitano spacewalking before his helmet problem

AMS-02

THE FUTURE OF SPACEWALKS

Today's spacewalks happen near Earth. But in the future, astronauts may travel to more distant places. They may return to the moon. They can repeat the slow, bouncing steps of Armstrong and Aldrin.

an artist's vision of a future base on the moon

Astronauts may visit asteroids. They could float around these giant rocks to study them and collect samples. They may also visit Mars. This planet's gravity is weaker than Earth's gravity and stronger than the moon's gravity. Wherever astronauts go, they will leave their spacecraft to explore.

GLOSSARY

air pressure force of air, often when it is pushing against the walls of a container holding it

asteroid rock that drifts through space

cosmonaut Russian astronaut

debris scattered pieces of something that has been broken or destroyed

gravity force that pulls objects towards the centre of Earth

hatch door of a spacecraft

Hubble Space Telescope telescope the size of a bus that circles Earth and takes pictures of distant stars

lander spacecraft designed to safely land on a moon or planet

module individual part of a space station

oxygen gas that people breathe to live

tether rope or cord that connects two objects together

thruster small engine that lets spacecraft move around in space

weightless not being pulled down towards Earth

COMPREHENSION QUESTIONS

1. How do space suits keep astronauts safe during spacewalks?

2. Look at the space suits on page 19. How have they changed over time?

3. Pages 24–27 describe some of the dangers of spacewalks. Does this description make you feel that spacewalks are worth the risks?

READ MORE

Space Pioneers (Story of Space), Steve Parker (Smart Apple Media, 2016).

The First Moon Walk (Incredible True Adventures), Ryan Nagelhout (Gareth Stevens Publishing, 2015).

Why Do Astronauts Wear Spacesuits? (Space Mysteries), Michael Portman (Gareth Stevens Publishing, 2013).

WEBSITES

BBC: Five Things about Tim Peake's Spacewalk
www.bbc.com/news/science-environment-35322257
Learn five important facts about Astronaut Tim Peake's spacewalk.

BBC: Tim Peake's First Spacewalk
www.bbc.com/news/live/science-environment-35303186
Watch Astronaut Tim Peake go on his first spacewalk.

ESA: 50 Years of Spacewalks
**www.esa.int/Our_Activities/Human_Spaceflight/
Highlights/50_years_of_spacewalks**
See pictures from the history of spacewalks.

INDEX